Pebble®
Bilingüe/ Plus
Bilingual

Ciencia física/Physical Science

La gravedad a nuestro alrededor/
Gravity All Around

por/by David Conrad

CAPSTONE PRESS
a capstone imprint

Pebble Plus is published by Capstone Press,
1710 Roe Crest Drive, North Mankato, Minnesota 56003.
www.capstonepub.com

Books published by Capstone Press are manufactured with paper containing at least 10 percent post-consumer waste.

Library of Congress Cataloging-in-Publication Data
Conrad, David (David J.), 1967–
  La gravedad a nuestro alrededor / por David Conrad = Gravity all around / by David Conrad.
  p. cm.—(Pebble plus bilingüe. Ciencia física = Pebble plus bilingual. Physical science)
  Includes index.
  Summary: "Simple text and color photographs introduce gravity, including its history and how it affects Earth—in both English and Spanish"—Provided by publisher.
  ISBN 978-1-4296-6906-1 (library binding)
  1. Gravity—Juvenile literature. 2. Gravitation—Juvenile literature. I. Title. II. Title: Gravity all around. III. Series.
QC178.C637418 2012
531'.14—dc22   2011000631

Editorial Credits

Gillia Olson, editor; Strictly Spanish, translation services; Veronica Correia, designer; Danielle Ceminsky, bilingual book designer; Eric Gohl, media researcher; Laura Manthe, production specialist

Photo Credits

The Bridgeman Art Library International/©Look and Learn/Private Collection/James Edwin McConnell, 13; The Royal Institution, London, UK/Robert Hannah, 15
Capstone Studio/Karon Dubke, cover, 9, 20–21 (all)
iStockphoto/posteriori, 5
Shutterstock/Andresr, 19 (boy on right); Blackbirds, 19 (background); Jacek Chabraszewski, 7; Mandy Godbehear, 1; Panos Karapanagiotis, 11; Ronald van der Beek, 17; Thomas M Perkins, 19 (boy on left)

Note to Parents and Teachers

The Ciencia física/Physical Science series supports national standards related to physical science. This book describes and illustrates gravity in both English and Spanish. The images support early readers in understanding the text. The repetition of words and phrases helps early readers learn new words. This book also introduces early readers to subject-specific vocabulary words, which are defined in the Glossary section. Early readers may need assistance to read some words and to use the Table of Contents, Glossary, Internet Sites, and Index sections of the book.

Printed in the United States of America in North Mankato, Minnesota.
062012
006762R

Table of Contents

Tabla de contenidos

What Is Gravity?

It makes a dropped glass
fall to the floor. It keeps bouncing
balls from flying off into space.
It's a force called gravity.

¿Qué es la gravedad?

Hace que un vaso golpeado se
caiga al piso. Evita que las pelotas
que rebotan no salgan volando
hacia el espacio. Es una fuerza
llamada gravedad.

Gravity can't be seen, but it's all around you. When you jump, gravity pulls you back to the ground.

No se puede ver a la gravedad, pero está en todas partes a tu alrededor. Cuando saltas, la gravedad te empuja hacia el suelo.

To see how gravity works, whirl a ball on a string. The string is like gravity. It keeps the ball from flying away. If the string breaks, the ball flies off.

Para ver cómo funciona la gravedad, gira una pelota atada a una cuerda. La cuerda es como la gravedad. Evita que la pelota salga volando. Si la cuerda se rompe, la pelota sale volando.

Proving Gravity

In the 300s BC, Aristotle of ancient Greece thought about why objects fell to the ground. He thought heavy things fell faster than light things.

Prueba de la gravedad

En los años 300 a. C., Aristóteles de Grecia antigua pensaba por qué los objetos se caían al suelo. Él pensaba que las cosas pesadas se caían más rápido que las cosas livianas.

People believed Aristotle until
the early 1600s. Then, Italian
scientist Galileo studied gravity.
He proved that all objects fall
at the same speed.

La gente le creyó a Aristóteles
hasta principios de 1600.
Entonces, el científico italiano
Galileo estudió la gravedad.
Él probó que todos los objetos
se caen a la misma velocidad.

In 1665 Sir Isaac Newton proved that gravity pulls all objects toward each other. He discovered that the moon circles Earth because of gravity.

En 1665, Sir Isaac Newton probó que la gravedad atrae todos los objetos unos a otros. Él descubrió que la Luna gira alrededor de la Tierra debido a la gravedad.

More or Less Gravity

If Earth had less gravity, it would
be like the moon. Earth would have
no water, air, plants, or animals.
They would all float away.

Más o menos gravedad

Si la Tierra tuviese menos
gravedad, sería como la Luna.
La Tierra no tendría agua, aire,
plantas o animales. Todos ellos
saldrían flotando.

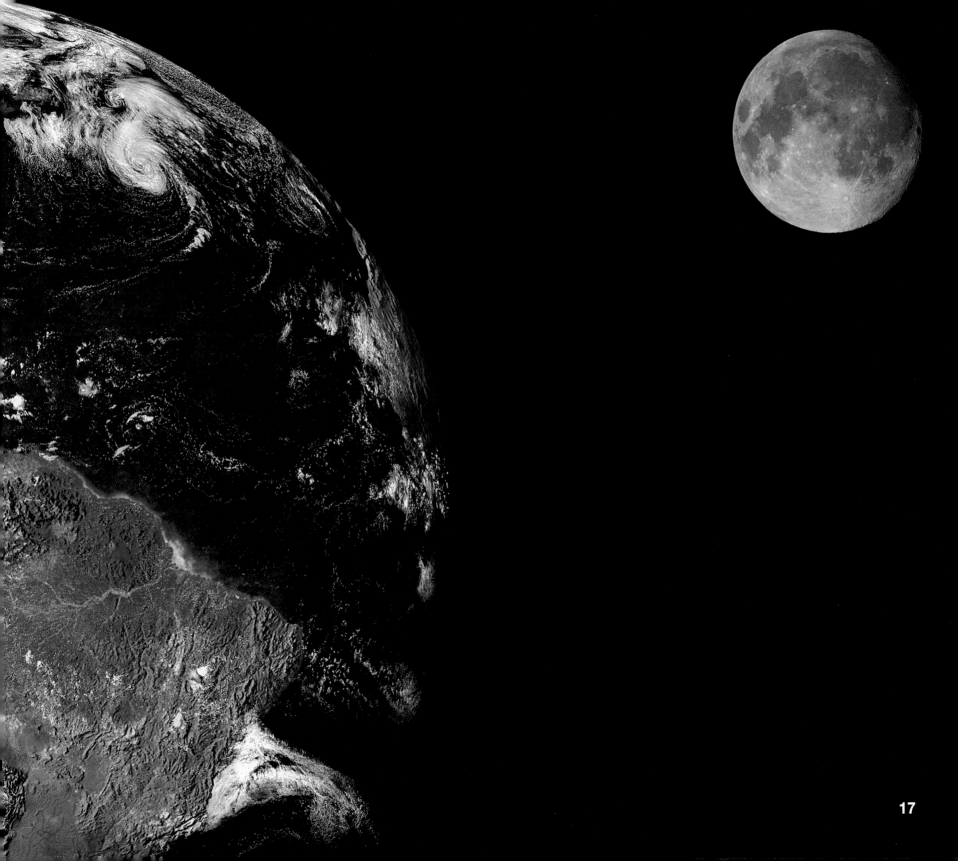

If Earth had more gravity, we would be as flat as pancakes on the ground. Imagine how different life would be if Earth had more or less gravity!

Si la Tierra tuviese más gravedad, nosotros estaríamos aplastados como panqueques en el piso. ¡Imagina qué diferente sería la vida si la Tierra tuviese más o menos gravedad!

Stronger than Gravity/Más fuerte que la gravedad

What You Need/Necesitas

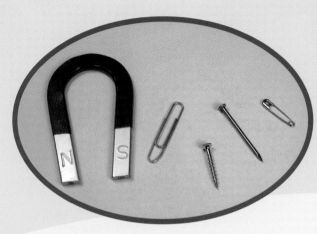

- 1 safety pin/1 imperdible
- 1 magnet/1 imán
- other small metal objects/ otros objetos pequeños de metal

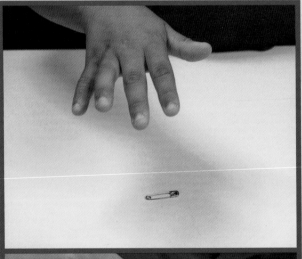

1

Drop a safety pin.
Gravity makes it fall.

Deja caer un imperdible.
La gravedad lo hace caer.

2

Hold the safety pin next to a magnet.
Then let it go. Try the other metal objects
too. What happens?

Sostén el imperdible cerca del imán.
Luego suéltalo. Prueba los otros objetos
de metal también. ¿Qué ocurre?

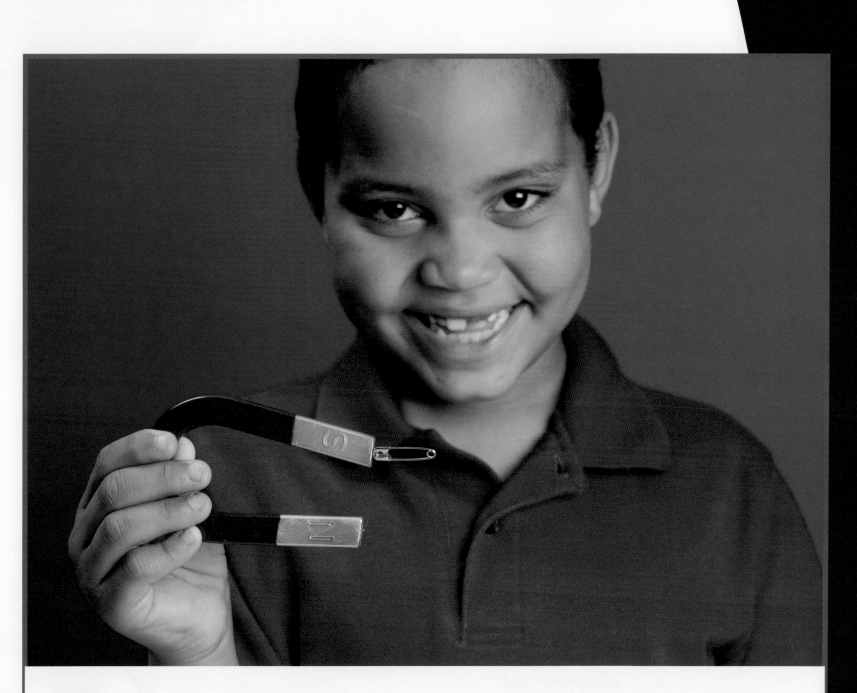

3 The metal objects stick to the magnet! The magnet is stronger than gravity.

¡Los objetos de metal se pegan al imán! El imán es más fuerte que la gravedad.

Glossary

ancient—belonging to a time long ago

discover—to find out about something

force—a power that causes something to change or move

gravity—the force that pulls all things to one another

speed—how fast or slow something moves

whirl—to turn in a circle

Internet Sites

FactHound offers a safe, fun way to find Internet sites related to this book. All of the sites on FactHound have been researched by our staff.

Here's all you do:

Visit *www.facthound.com*

Type in this code: 9781429669061

Check out projects, games and lots more at
www.capstonekids.com

Glosario

antigua—perteneciente a un periodo que pasó hace mucho tiempo

descubrir—averiguar acerca de algo

la fuerza—un poder que causa que algo cambie o se mueva

girar—dar vueltas en un círculo

la gravedad—la fuerza que atrae todas las cosas entre sí

la velocidad—qué rápido o despacio algo se mueve

Sitios de Internet

FactHound brinda una forma segura y divertida de encontrar sitios de Internet relacionados con este libro. Todos los sitios en FactHound han sido investigados por nuestro personal.

Esto es todo lo que tienes que hacer:

Visita *www.facthound.com*

Ingresa este código: 9781429669061

¡Algo súper divertido! Hay proyectos, juegos y mucho más en **www.capstonekids.com**

Index

Índice